75¢

S H A K E S P E A R E ' S
T H E A T R E

Coward, McCann & Geoghegan, Inc.   New York

SHAKESPEARE'S
THEATRE

Written and illustrated by

C. WALTER HODGES

To

C L A R E

The author thanks Encyclopedia Britannica Films Inc.
for permission to reproduce many of the illustrations in this book.

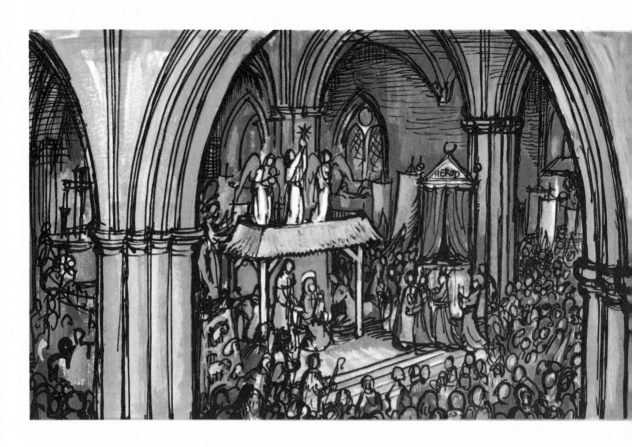

I

Watching the television screen not long ago I saw a film about Australian aborigines, the most primitive race on earth, who still live today as people used to live in the Stone Age. They were performing two of their magic dances. In the first of these a man pretended to be a snake. He was supposed to be the Divine Snake who is the totem of his tribe. A whole morning had been spent dressing him up for the part. His hair was stiffened and shaped out with twigs, and this and all his body was covered with clay and seeds, making a thick white pattern on his black skin. When at

5

last he was ready he sat cross-legged on the ground while the other men in the ritual stood round him, weirdly chanting, and prodding him lightly with sticks. Whenever he was touched, the Snake-man wriggled and shuffled about a little, as a disturbed snake might do. That was all that seemed to happen. In the other dance a number of men were pretending to be kangaroos. They too, squatted on the ground. They munched at plants and sometimes sat up making look-around movements, like grazing kangaroos. The other men crept up stealthily behind them and pretended to strike them with their spears. The Kangaroo-men then rolled about on the ground as if they had been killed. That, too, was all that seemed to happen. The men in both these ritual plays were gaunt, bearded, senior-looking people. It seemed rather ridiculous that they should be getting up to such antics at their age.

A few nights later on the same television screen I saw a mature and well-educated Englishman pretending to be Julius Caesar. He had been dressed up very carefully in clothes which were supposed to make him look like a Roman patrician of some two thousand years ago. After a little while a number of other men in similar clothes gathered round and pretended to stick knives into him, and he then rolled on the ground and pretended to be dead. I knew that when the cameras moved off him, the man who had acted the part of Julius Caesar would get up and go away to a dressing room, wash the paint off his face, put on his ordinary clothes, and go out into the street and call a taxi. He was, I suppose, a man of about the same age as the Snake- and Kangaroo-men, yet the play of *Julius Caesar* did not seem at all ridiculous, as the animal plays of the other men had done. Of course this was partly because *Julius Caesar* had been composed for civilized people like ourselves by a great poet, William Shakespeare, less than four hundred years ago, while the other plays belonged to the distant pre-history of the

6

human race. Yet still on the whole the similarities between the two kinds of play are more striking than the differences. All were mere pretences; all were supposed to represent important events, and in each case the players were very serious about what they were doing. Indeed, if anything, the Snake- and Kangaroo-men could be said to be more serious than the actors in *Julius Caesar*. The Snake-man believed it was very important for all his tribe that their snake totem should be seen to be alive and able to possess the body of a

man with its spirit; the Kangaroo-men believed that by their imitation of a successful hunt, the real hunt that was to follow would be made successful, and provide food for all their village; whereas the Shakespearean actor might only be hoping that he had given a good performance, and that his audience would think well of him. The drama of the primitive men seemed to be concerned entirely with matters of ritual and religion affecting their community, while the civilized actor was concerned mainly with acting for its own sake. But this is still not entirely true. In fact, the basis of all theatrical art is eventually concerned in one way or another with religion or morality, and one does not have to go very far back in the history of any branch of the theatre to find its religious beginnings.

During the boyhood of William Shakespeare, the acting which
he knew, indeed almost the only kind of acting which at that time
existed in England, was a form of the same religious drama, presented mainly by amateur players, which had been devised by the
priests of the Church for the teaching of their Christian communities
hundreds of years before. And side by side with this there also
existed another, even earlier, form of religious drama, though at
first sight it might appear not at all religious, nor even very dramatic.
The ancient rituals with which our pagan ancestors had celebrated

9

the seasons of the sun and moon and the sowing and reaping of the corn had survived as folk games and dances. Perhaps the most popular of these survivals in Shakespeare's time were the festivities of early summer, the dancing round the May-Pole and the crowning of the May Queen. The picture shows this ceremony as it might have looked in the early Middle Ages. Boys and girls are dancing round the May-Pole, binding it with green leaves and ropes of straw. In the background can be seen the May Queen throned in an arbour, and at her side the Jack-in-the-Green who is dressed all over in a covering of leaves on a wicker frame. He represents the god or spirit of summer. That such festivals were the relics of an ancient pagan religion was well understood by disapproving preachers in Shakespeare's time, one of whom wrote of the May-Pole that the people 'dance about it like as the heathen people did at the dedication of the Idols, whereof this is a perfect pattern, or rather the thing itself.'

Dancing round the May-pole in the early Middle Ages. In the background is the May Queen, and at her side the Jack-in-the-Green.

11

A travelling troupe of puppet players, jugglers, tight-rope
walkers, clowns and other players.

The May-Pole dancers and the 'Mummers', such as the Jack-in-
the-Green, were all, of course, friends and neighbours dressed up
for the occasion. They were, as we say, amateurs. But often when
they went to the great fairs, which were among the principal holiday
occasions of medieval life, they would see there the jugglers and

tight-rope walkers, the ballad-singers, clowns and puppet-players who used to go about in small troupes from fair to fair and from country to country. These were the first professionals in our story. They lived by their skill as individual performers. But they did not perform 'plays' in our sense of the word. This in early times was left to the amateurs.

The earliest known plays of the Middle Ages were composed by priests and acted by them before the congregation in church, during the service, at important festivals of the Christian year, to illustrate as vividly as possible the story and teaching of Christ. They were very short plays. The picture shows one that was performed at Easter. An empty tomb is set before the altar steps. Two young priests dressed as angels stand beside it, and they are met by three others who are supposed to be the three holy women who went early to the tomb of Christ on the first Easter morning. 'Whom do ye seek in the sepulchre?' asks one of the angels. 'We seek Jesus of Nazareth, who was crucified,' reply the women. 'He is not here: he is risen,' say the angels, and they take the folded grave-clothes from the empty tomb and hold them up to show. The priests representing the three women then turn to the congregation and announce the Resurrection, and all the people join in the singing of the *Te Deum,* while the church bells begin to ring. This little episode is the first written play surviving in England. The idea was at once so effective and so popular that it was soon extended, and other parts of the Easter story were treated in the

14

same way; Mary Magdalene's meeting with the risen Christ whom she mistakes for the gardener; or, an imaginary scene made vivid by its reference to everyday life, the three Marys stopping to buy spices at a market stall, on their way to the tomb. So also at Christmas the church services were celebrated with little plays showing the shepherds arriving at the manger, the journey of the Magi, and the villainous Herod raging with hatred at the news of the birth

The play 'The Three Marys at the Sepulchre' performed at Easter by priests before the altar steps.

A play being performed outside a great cathedral.

of Christ the King. The simple settings for these plays, the manger, Herod's throne, a Heaven for the angelic choir, were arranged conveniently in different parts of the church, but as time went on there was so much being done, with so many actors needed and so many people crowding to watch, that there was no longer room enough in the churches, and it was found more convenient to mount the plays outside. In the picture above we show a play taking place outside the West Front of a great cathedral. A long stage or platform has been erected so that the actors are raised up and can be clearly seen by all the audience standing below. The scene at present being acted is Christ brought before Pilate, who is washing his hands. But also on the stage are actors and properties belonging to other parts of the story: on the left is God the Father seated above in a sun-like 'glory', representing Heaven. Below this is a table for the scene of the Last Supper. A little to the right of it, a green-painted 'hill', representing the Mount of Olives. On the right of the picture are the post to which Christ will be tied, with the scourge for His whipping; and the cross for the crucifixion afterwards. Between these we see the actor who plays Satan. Perversely, the Devil and his friends soon established themselves among the more popular characters, and have remained so in one form or another almost to our own day. The Devil quickly found a way of making himself less frightening than was originally intended; he became a comedian.

By this time an important change had taken place in the acting of these plays. They were no longer performed only by the priests. With so many parts needed, the people of the parish had had to be called in to lend a hand, and they brought with them their own ideas, some of which were borrowed from the ancient mummers' plays and pagan festivals. These things the priests had never entirely succeeded in stamping out, so instead they allowed them and adapted them to their own purposes. But at this point medieval drama, having come out of the Churches and into the street, though it remained religious in its themes, and still existed under the

Pope Urban IV inaugurates Corpus Christi.

patronage of the Church, began to be more and more secular in its methods.

In the year 1264, three hundred years before Shakespeare was born, Pope Urban IV established the feast of Corpus Christi, and this day in June, when the weather is fine and the hours of daylight long, soon became the greatest day of the year for the dramatic festivals of the Church. All the day from dawn to sunset would be given over to the enactment of the Bible story, in towns all over Europe.

19

Here we see a play being performed in the market-place of a European town in the fifteenth century. In this case it is an imaginary

A play performed in the market place of a European town in the fifteenth century. The central theme is of St. Michael and the Angels fighting the hosts of Satan who are issuing from the mouth of Hell. In the foreground is Herod on his throne. An imaginary setting based on the idea of the Lucerne play in Nicoll.

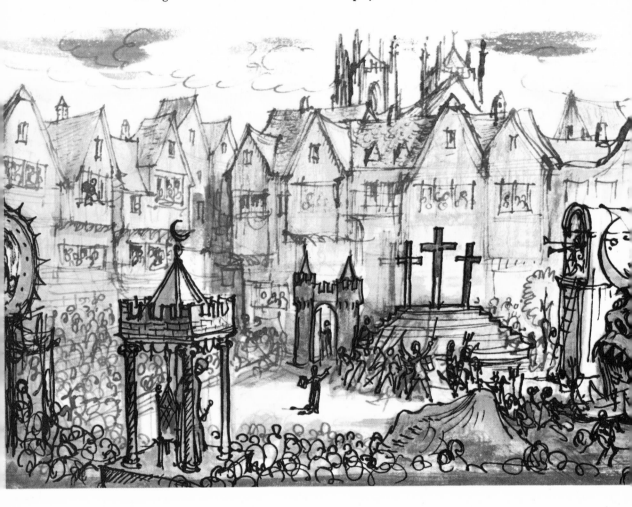

scene, but it corresponds closely to performances that actually were done in just this way. The method of staging is similar to that which we saw in front of the cathedral on page 16, but it is enlarged and extended. All the parts of the setting were in position in the market-place when the people of the audience arrived in the early morning and took their places on the stands and at the windows all around. In the sketch you can see God the Father raised up in Heaven on the extreme left. Next is King Herod under a sort of canopy with a crescent on the top of it, to show that he was a sort of Eastern Pagan, like the Mahommedans, and therefore (in those days) obviously wicked. At the extreme right is the great Hell Mouth. This favourite piece of scenery is represented again and again in the plays and paintings of the Middle Ages and even later. Out of it we see the devils running, to be met by St. Michael and the angels in battle. Beyond the Hell Mouth is a high place under a canopy, which is Heaven, with a ladder down which the angels descend. Next to it is the hill of Calvary with its three crosses; and to the left of that a city gate, representing the gate of Jerusalem for the episode of Christ's entry on Palm Sunday. A man in a black robe stands in the midst of it all and explains to the audience what is going on. He is what became known in later times as a Presenter. The various localities of the drama here set around the market place were usually known as 'mansions'. In the great Passion Play given in the city of Mons in 1501 there were sixty-seven of these mansions. The play took four days to perform, and forty-eight days to rehearse.

Since of course it needed a very great number of actors to perform all the plays of the Bible story in the elaborate way that was developed as time went on, a system arose whereby the various incidents were allotted to various sections of the community; usually, in a big town, to the various trade and craftsman's Guilds.

Diagram of a medieval town showing the Guilds grouped
together in districts.

In a medieval town there was a natural tendency for the different
trades to group together in districts, and here we show an imaginary
diagram of such a town and its Guilds, with, next door to it, a
representation of the different incidents which the Guildsmen
portrayed in the town's Corpus Christi play. You will see that there
was often a connexion between the nature of the trade and the
incident it represented. Thus the Bakers presented the Last Supper,
and Shoemakers the long journey of the Flight into Egypt, and the

22

A representation of the different incidents which the Guildsmen portrayed in the town's Corpus Christi play.

Masons and Carpenters the building of the Temple. The Smiths performed David and Goliath, the Butchers the Crucifixion, the Goldsmiths the Three Magi with their gifts. The Shipwrights would present Noah's Ark; Fishmongers the Calling of St. Peter; Grocers, who sold sweets and spices, presented Adam and Eve and the forbidden fruit; Weavers, the Resurrection; and the Tailors and Milliners, the Harrowing of Hell (which will be explained later). The Guildsmen were very proud of their plays and their parts in them, and handed them on from one generation to the next, as they still do in the Passion Play in the little town of Oberammergau in Germany to this day. In England, in Shakespeare's time, there were still performed in York, Wakefield, Coventry, Chester and other places a great many series of plays of this kind. They are known as Mystery Plays or Miracle Plays. Many collections of them still exist, handed down to us from the Middle Ages, together with records of accounts, plans of the layout of playing places and many other fascinating internal details of these events. We read of the money spent for a pound of hemp to mend the angels' wigs; of a new coat and a pair of hose for the Archangel Gabriel; of Adam and Eve 'apparelled in white leather'—which was presumably meant to represent skin, since their costume also required 'fig leaves'; we read of clouds and thunderbolts; of 'fayre trees', fountains, and fine flowers for a Paradise scene; and of the three shillings and fourpence that was 'paid to ye mynstrells of Corpus Christi Playe'.

Here, then, in the next picture is a scene in a tradesman's house early on Corpus Christi morning. He is dressed for his part as King Herod, and his family are making a few last-minute adjustments to his costume. His next door neighbour, one of the devils from Hell Mouth, has called to tell him to hurry. They will be fined by their Guild if they are late.

The method of play-presentation with 'mansions' seems to have remained in standard theatrical practice right down to Shakespeare's time and even, it is thought, in some of his own plays. But in

A grocer prepares for his part of Herod on Corpus Christi morning.

25

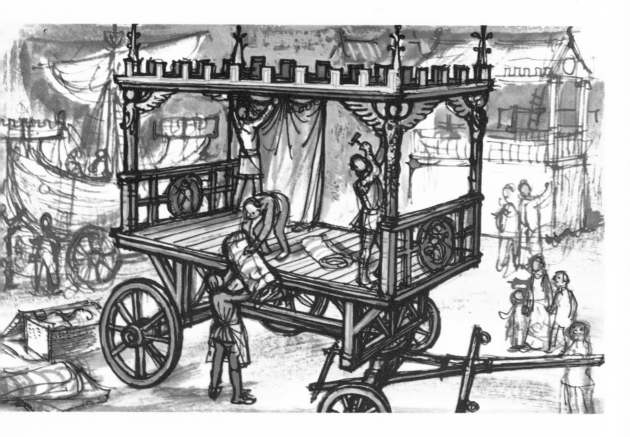

A Pageant built high off the ground to allow the actors to
get underneath to change their costumes.

England in the late Middle Ages there was developed from this
another form of stage, mounted on a great wagon called a 'Pageant',
which could be pulled through the streets of a town in procession,
so that the episode for which it was built could be acted at different
stopping-places along the route of the procession. Nobody knows
exactly what these 'Pageants' looked like, and they were certainly
of many kinds. On this page we have imagined one of them being
got ready, a few days before the play. It is built high off the ground
so that the underneath of it, closed in with hangings, can be used

as a changing-room by the actors, and the front wheels have been made so that they can turn fairly sharply to negotiate the street corners of the crowded town. In the background can be seen two other Pageants, one of which is Noah's ship. In the next picture we see these Pageants in the procession. The one that was being got ready, now draped, is in the middle. Perhaps that is Pontius Pilate seated in it. In the foreground is a tableau of the Resurrection. It is likely that in some towns a procession like this was given on one day, and the plays themselves on the day following.

Pageants in procession. The one in the foreground represents the Resurrection with the soldiers asleep.

Here is the Pageant of the Harrowing of Hell. The story is that between the times of the Crucifixion and the Resurrection, Christ descended into Hell to rescue the souls of those good people who, having been born before He came on earth to redeem them, now lay

A scene from the Harrowing of Hell.

in the Devil's power for no fault of their own. So Christ comes
to Hell Mouth, saying:

> 'Princes of Hell open your gate,
> And let my folk forth go;
> The Prince of Peace comes in his state,
> Whether ye will or no.'

He calls forth Moses, David, Isaiah and others; but first he calls
Adam and Eve, the father and mother of us all, who are here shown
kneeling, robed in white. The demons of Hell are at last powerless
to hold them any longer.

Plays were probably performed in the Pageants and in the streets also. This shows a scene from the Massacre of the Innocents with Herod seated above. Other Pageants can be seen in the background waiting their turn to come before the audience. Scaffolds have been put up for a big audience.

At certain prepared places along the way the audiences would be waiting for the Pageants to come up, each in turn with its play. Above is the scene of the Massacre of the Innocents. King Herod sits above in the Pageant and watches his soldiery in the street below carrying out his bloodthirsty command. Herod was traditionally shown as a ranting tyrant. 'Herod rages in the Pageant and in the street also' is written as an instruction in one of these plays. We have here shown a ladder so that King Herod can come down and rage in the street.

The episode of Noah's Ark was one of the most popular. In this it was a tradition for Mrs. Noah to be represented as a cantankerous old thing who would not go into the ark until she was dragged in by force by Shem, Ham and Japhet; but not before (as shown here) she had given Noah a box on the ears.

A scene from the Chester play of the Deluge.

It may be seen that as time went on the religious nature of these Miracle plays has become more and more mixed up with popular, imaginary, and comic characters and ideas. Mrs. Noah, the Shepherds at Bethlehem, King Herod, and especially the Devil and his minions, these and others of the kind became such favourites with the citizen audiences that their parts were continually being increased in scope. The Church which had originally sponsored the plays did not approve of this turn of events, but could now do little to stop it, for the Church no longer paid the bill. The plays had grown so costly, not only in money but in manpower, that they had now to be managed and paid for by the Town Councils, which, much as they may have respected the Church, saw their duty to their citizens in a rather different light. On high days and holidays the people looked for entertainment as well as teaching, and the Town Councils saw no reason why the two should not be mixed. The influence of the lay people increased as the clergy withdrew their patronage; and so the nature of play-acting began to change.

A new kind of play began to be seen. It was called a Moral Interlude, or Morality. Its themes were not taken from the Bible story, but were composed to teach the moral and religious duties of human beings, and its characters were impersonations of human virtues and vices. As usual, the vices quickly established themselves with all the favourite and most amusing acting parts, and a comic devil known as the Vice was a well-known character of the English stage even in Shakespeare's time.

In our next picture we see a Morality play called *The Castle of Perseverance,* as it was performed probably near Lincoln in the middle of the fifteenth century. Here we also see a different method of staging, for the pageant method, though convenient and very popular in English towns, was not the only one. The 'mansions' or 'houses', instead of being mounted on wagons and rolled

32

The Morality play 'The Castle of Perseverance' being performed near
Lincoln. (Based on the reconstruction by Dr. Richard Southern.)

through the streets, are here brought all together into a round
'Theatre', an enclosure specially dug and fenced off for the purpose,
and inside it the actors and their audience are all, as it were, mixed
together. The different mansions, here severally inhabited by God,
Covetousness, the Flesh and the Devil and others, are set around

on the outside of the Circle. In the centre is the Castle of Perseverance itself, with Mankind and his bed underneath the Castle. For the different incidents of the play the audience had to turn about, facing first one direction and then another, and special officers were appointed to keep the ways clear and keep everything going without confusion.

A triumphal arch.

As time went on the scenic arrangements for such performances became very elaborate and gay; particularly when they were put on, as often happened, for the entertainment of princes. When Kings were crowned, or returned victorious from the wars, or paid state visits to each other, they would be welcomed into the cities with processions and displays of extravagant splendour. In the streets, magnificent triumphal arches would be built, made of wood and canvas and plaster, but modelled and painted by skilled artists. Musicians placed over the archways among the flags and statues played triumphal music, and the visiting prince was met by actors in fine costumes, who recited poems of welcome written to grace the occasion by poets of renown. Shakespeare himself may have seen the splendid reception given for Queen Elizabeth by the Earl of Leicester when the Queen visited Kenilworth in 1575. Shakespeare was then a boy of eleven. In later years he himself took part in the celebrations of great magnificence which welcomed James I through the streets of London.

So far, all the various forms of drama we have been discussing have been played and managed almost entirely by amateurs, though here and there, as time went on, a few professionals might occasionally have been called in to lend a hand. The professionals, whom we saw as jugglers and tight-rope walkers at the fairground in our picture on page 12, had an unbroken tradition that went back to the days of ancient Rome. In the Middle Ages they had become Jongleurs and Troubadours. Now, however, as the Middle Ages drew to a close, some of them were beginning to form companies with a repertory of short plays or 'interludes' as part of their stock-in-trade. It is thought that many of the non-religious parts found in the later Miracle Plays may have been introduced by the professionals who were employed to help on these occasions. For the most part, until Shakespeare's time, the professionals continued

Actors on the road.

as they always had done, tramping the roads from town to town, carrying their gear in a cart in all sorts of weather. They were not always welcome. They were looked upon as vagabonds, 'masterless men' who had no proper trade, and were therefore likely to be thieves and 'sturdy beggars'. In our picture on the next page we see one such company being turned away at the town gate by the constable.

Players being turned away at the town gate.

But the great lords, who for their own reasons appreciated the value of skilled entertainment, eventually lent their patronage to some of the better companies, who thus were able to travel the country as The Earl of Leicester's Men, the Lord Admiral's Men, and the like. This gave them status, as we say, but it did not happen to any great degree much before Shakespeare's time.

37

A play being presented at the house of a nobleman.

In this picture we see our company of actors entertaining the guests at dinner in a nobleman's hall, with a play about a jealous husband. And in the next picture we see them on the road again, this time entertaining the crowds outside a country inn. Notice their stage, which is a very simple affair of boards laid upon trestles,

38

with an enclosure of curtains at the back. This stage they can carry about with them in their cart. It is the simplest, the oldest and the most universal form of stage in the world, and we shall see later in this book how it was used in one of the world's most famous theatres. There is a phrase about actors being 'upon the boards'.

Actors putting on a show outside a country inn.

Here in the next picture we see our travelling company upon their boards again, in a scene from an early farce called *Ralph Roister Doister,* which was written in about the year 1550, fourteen years before Shakespeare was born. In this scene a character called Matthew Merrygreeke and his friends are trying to arrange a marriage between the bragging Ralph Roister Doister and old Madge Mumblecrust, the nurse. Matthew is describing Ralph's exploits. 'Yea,' he says, 'and the last time he saw an elephant, he starts out of a bush and with pure strength of arms plucks out his great tusk!' 'Lor!' exclaims Madge, 'what a thing that was!' 'Yea, but, Merrygreeke,' says Ralph, breaking in, 'do not forget the *other* elephant, the one that fled away!'

The comedy over, and after a night spent perhaps in a loft behind the inn, next morning the company will be on the road again. We will imagine that it is late summer and they are on their way to London, where they hope to find shelter and audiences to see them through the winter. They plan to set up their stage in one of the great inns in the City. They are not alone in this idea. London is

A scene from Ralph Roister Doister.

like a magnet for all the players' companies in the country, and the inns are their usual play-houses. Here, then, they have arrived on Highgate Hill, where, long before, Dick Whittington had paused to listen to the bells of London, in sight of the tall spire of Old St. Paul's. The spire was burnt down in 1561 and never rebuilt, so we will date this picture for September 1560, three years and six months before Shakespeare was born.

Players entering London by Highgate Hill.

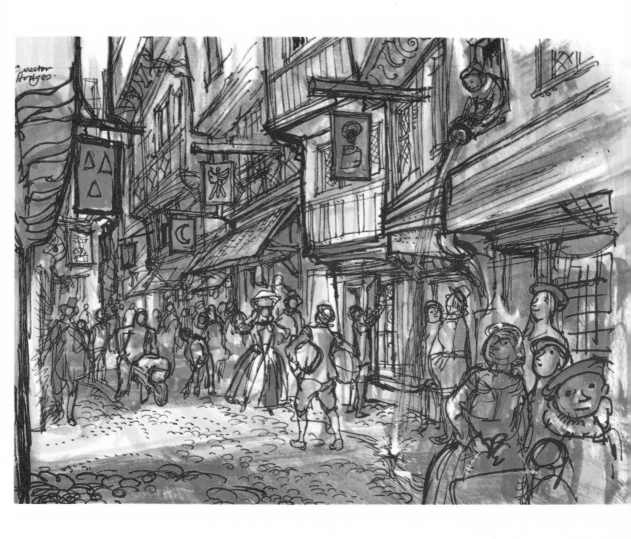

II

Imagine now the city of London in the late 1560's. Most of its streets are noisy and narrow and stink too frequently of the sewage in the foul gutters, as we have so often been told. But the crowds that move here are of a new kind of people. The Middle Ages are long over. In the distant country towns, it is true, the old way of

43

life continues much as before, as, for example, in the keeping on
with the old traditional Guild or Mystery Plays. In Chester and
Coventry the amateurs are still playing Noah and Moses and
Pontius Pilate on Corpus Christi Day. But to London now come all
the literate and sophisticated people of the English Renaissance.
In London the grocer's apprentice has begun to read books for
pleasure. In London the booksellers thrive. In London there is a
large public with a continual desire for the stretching of its faculty
for imagination, which is as much as to say, in modern terms, a
public for the theatre. And so to London, as we have seen, come the
professionals, to earn money by satisfying the need.

44

Here, below, is a picture in which we look down into the yard of a London inn, where our players' company has now set up its stage, the same little stage which we saw in the country a few pages back. There were many inns which were used like this, some of them almost permanently, with stages probably indoors as well as out. But notice how the crowds are thronging round. And in the next

The crowd outside the inn-yard.

picture notice what sort of crowds they were. They were not always, at these public playing places, the quietest or most seemly kind of people. It turned out that beggars, bullies, pickpockets and drunk-ards were as fond of entertainment as ladies and gentlemen were, a fact which Town Councils and other administrative bodies have always found quite reasonably to be a nuisance. In any case, administrative bodies are never really very fond of acting, or of the sometimes rather unruly people who do it. Acting of any kind is not always logical or reasonable; it is sometimes difficult to know how to take it seriously; and administrators are very often serious-minded and cautious people whose job it is to make and keep proper rules for everybody's good. The Lord Mayor and the Corporation of the City of London therefore were not at all pleased with the coming and conduct of the players in London, and made as many rules as they could to keep them away. Had it not been for Queen Elizabeth I and her courtiers, whose way of life had more time for players and who understood them better, the Corporation of London might have succeeded in prohibiting plays and players altogether. As it was, the Queen and her Court did all they could to patronize and protect the more reputable player companies, 'for the recreation of our loving subjects, and for our solace and pleasure when we shall please to see them'. Even so, the Corporation made things hard enough for them, and to avoid some of their difficulties the players tended more and more to set up their stages not in the City itself, but just outside, where the Lord Mayor had less control.

James Burbage and his portable stage.

Prominent in one of the Companies, the Earl of Leicester's Men, was an actor named James Burbage who had once been a carpenter. We see him here turning over in his mind a new idea. He is leaning against his familiar portable stage with its trestles and its curtained enclosure at the back, which is being erected in a field near London. Two boys of his company are busy studying their parts. In the background can be seen the players' cart carrying the flag of the Earl of Leicester, whose emblem is a bear chained to a post. Perhaps it was this bear which helped to give James Burbage his idea. On the south bank of the river Thames there were at that time two round wooden buildings, not unlike the theatre for the Castle of Perseverance on p. 33, which were kept for the sports of bull and bear baiting. These sports were brutal and I shall not describe them. But they were also very paying games, and the owners of the buildings made money. It occurred to James Burbage that a permanent building kept for putting on plays might be equally

Bear-baiting.

rewarding, or, if all else failed, this too could be used for baiting bulls and bears. Accordingly he discussed the idea with some friends and drew up a plan, and found financial backing, and in the year 1576 there began to be built the first permanent professional public play-house of the modern world. Burbage called it the 'Theatre'. A 'theatre' is a 'place where action goes on', as in an operating theatre or a 'theatre of war'. In Burbage's Theatre the action was acting. It was the first time in England a building had been called this, for that purpose.

James Burbage plans a permanent theatre.

The first permanent public playhouse in course of construction.

We do not know for certain what the Theatre looked like, and this is not the sort of book to go into argumentative details, but the details we shall give of this and of The Globe, the playhouse which followed it, are based upon logical argument and may for most general purposes be trusted. The variations you may observe represent some of the different possibilities available in imaginative reconstruction.

51

Inside the playhouse, with a portable stage in position.

The Theatre was a building with a wooden framework forming a circular enclosure around an open courtyard. In this courtyard stood the stage. At first it may have been a stage differing very little from the one James Burbage and other actors used on their travels and in the inns, though perhaps slightly more elaborate, like the one shown on this page. This would have been useful because it could have been cleared away if at any time the yard was needed as an arena for bear-baiting or the like. Around the yard were three galleries, one above the other, with seats for the spectators. There were no seats in the yard itself: here the audience had to stand.

Nor was there ever a roof over the yard. Later on when the stage became permanent, this had a roof built over it. On this page we see a view of the auditorium taken from the stage. Notice the three spectator galleries, the yard, the two pillars which hold up the stage roof, and the main entrance, through which some children are peeping to see what's going on. What is going on in fact is a management discussion about shares in the gate money.

A view of the auditorium taken from the permanent stage.

The stage of the new theatre with its thatched roof.

Here now is a view from the other direction, showing all the
stage. It is a very plain stage. The roof over it is thatched, though
the posts which support it are elaborate and make a handsome show.
The stage itself is a high one, which is necessary if the people standing in the yard are to have a clear view of the play, and it is hung all

54

round with a great skirt of cloth, closing it in underneath. There would be several sets of these hangings, in different colours and patterns to suit the moods of different plays. Thus, for tragic plays, black hangings were usual; comedies, histories or pastoral plays might use red, white or green. At the back of the stage are two doors, which lead into the 'tiring-house' where the actors attire themselves—what is today called 'back-stage'. The doors are large, so that scenic properties can be carried through. Scenery itself, as we know it today, could not of course be used on such a stage, but this does not mean that there was no other sort of spectacle. There was much. The scenic ideas inherited from the old Mystery Plays, and painted scenic constructions of the kind used for royal parades and triumphal arches were all available and often used.

There still exists a playhouse inventory of that time which lists trees, thrones, tombs, chariots and the like, and there is a description of a play set with many thrones, a Hell Mouth, a castle, a gibbet, banners and streamers and over all, the painted canopy of Heaven. Painted and dressed and hung with tapestries, therefore, this stage could be as gay as ever need be; but here for the present we see it plain.

Above the two doors there is a gallery with windows. This could be used either for spectators (who seem not to have minded much whether they saw the show from the front or the back) or for musicians, or very often for actors in special scenes in a play. This back wall of the stage, the frontage of the tiring-house, is very similar to the screen wall at the entrance to the great halls of Tudor noblemen's houses. A simple one of these screens has been seen in the picture on page 54, but many also have windows above, as here in the Theatre, though usually they are more ornate. In all cases there are two doors like this. The actors must have used these screens as a background for their plays time and time again during their travels.

The scenic ideas of the Mystery Plays were often used on
the Elizabethan stage.

It may have been to this Theatre, then, built by James Burbage at Shoreditch in the fields just outside the northern gate of the city, that Shakespeare found his way when as a young man he first came to London. Or he may have gone to one of the playhouses more recently built, again just outside the city limits, on the south bank of the Thames. Burbage's enterprise in Shoreditch had proved very successful, and other managers had been quick to follow his lead. This view shows among other things the number of playhouses that were flourishing in London in the year 1600. Notice that the principal group of them is on the south bank, the district that was, then as now, called Bankside. In this view, however, you will not see Burbage's Theatre in Shoreditch. It had stood next-door to The Curtain playhouse (the first to be built after it) but in 1598 it was pulled down and rebuilt presumably with improvements, on Bankside.

St Paul's Cathedral

BANKSIDE

The Bear Ring

The Rose

The Globe

The Swan

The Curtain

SHOREDITCH

Bishopsgate
Street

HOUNDSDITCH

FIELDS

The Tower
of London

Billingsgate

Southwark Cathedral

SOUTHWARK

The Globe.

It was renamed The Globe. Here we see it. A performance is due to begin, but people are still pushing in past the hucksters at the entrance. Round at the back is the tiring-house door, and nearby you can see one or two bits of stage property leaning against the wall. The part of the building that juts out on the left is the housing for a staircase. There is another in the same position on the far side. In the background is old London Bridge and, beyond it, the Tower of London. On the extreme right is the great church of St. Mary Overie, now Southwark Cathedral, where one of Shakespeare's brothers, an actor, lies buried.

A rehearsal in progress on the stage
of The Globe.

The great fame of The Globe playhouse is that here Shakespeare
worked and wrote, and acted in his own plays. Of this playhouse
he became part-owner. Old James Burbage had died in 1597, but
his son Richard had taken over from him, and was the most famous
actor of his day. It was he who on the stage of The Globe first acted
the parts of Hamlet, Othello and King Lear. For a moment we

62

have a glimpse of a rehearsal in progress on the stage of The Globe, fairly early in the morning before the sun has risen high enough to shine down into the empty galleries. The play is a revival of *Romeo and Juliet,* the scene at the beginning where the Montagues and Capulets meet. Shakespeare himself is conducting the rehearsal, from the table in the foreground.

Bad weather means no performance.

Here we may visualize two even earlier moments of that day. In the first, just at dawn, the man who looks after the place, and sleeps, probably, in the tiring-house has just come out into the yard and finds that it is raining. If the rain persists there will be no play that day, for in bad weather there is no shelter for the spectators in the yard, and not very much for those in the galleries, except at the back. The actors and stage-furniture would be protected in a light rain by the stage roof. However, in the next picture, at sunrise,

A view across fields to The Globe with, to the left, a neighbouring playhouse, The Rose.

the rain has cleared away, and the day promises to be fine. The view is from the south-west across the fields, which in those days came almost to the river, and it shows The Globe with, to the left, a neighbouring playhouse, The Rose, which was under the rival management of one Philip Henslowe. A glimpse of the river can be seen between the two playhouses. In the background we see again the tower of St. Mary Overie, and, to the left of it, the high roof of the hall of the Bishop of Winchester's palace. Over both the play-

65

A flag is hoisted to show that a performance will take place.

66

houses the flagpoles are still bare, but soon, at The Globe, now that the day is clear, a man will climb the stairs to the turret to hoist the flag. This was the usual sign that there would be a performance that afternoon. Every playhouse had its flag, which could be seen by the people in the city streets across the river. Here on some previous day notices would have been pasted up, advertising the plays to be performed. Plays were not put on for a run, as they are nowadays. Two or three consecutive performances of one play would be exceptional. There were many revivals of established favourites; but new plays, needless to say, were always the great attraction, and for these the entrance fee was usually doubled. Here we now see the play bills being posted at the southern end of old London Bridge. We are looking across the Bridge between the shops

Playbills being posted.

One way to The Globe lay over London Bridge.

and houses that crowded its length on either side. Through this lane, soon after one o'clock, people will begin pushing their way to get to the playhouse in good time to find a comfortable position where they can see and hear well. Many others will be coming over by

Another way to The Globe. The Thames watermen carry
the audience across the river. A rival playhouse, The Rose,
is seen in the foreground.

boat. Like taxis at theatre-time today, before and after the play the
Thames watermen will be gathered at the landing stages in their

dozens to pick up customers. Now we see them landing at Bankside, the people making their way up the wooden causeway over the mud, because it is low tide. The playhouses shown are the Globe (on the left), the Rose, and, on the right, with no flag flying, the bear-baiting ring.

One entered The Globe as a rule through the main entrance, though certain privileged people were admitted by way of the tiring-house door at the back. These people would pay the highest prices to be allowed to sit in the gallery over the stage, or even sometimes upon the stage itself where, according to one writer of the time, they were often a nuisance, not so much because they took up too much room on the stage (it was a large stage and there was room to spare) as because by talking and playing cards and showing off their clothes they drew too much attention to themselves and to their dandified bad manners. But the ordinary people going in at the main gate would pay one penny (probably worth about a shilling of our money) to a man who stood there with a box, and for this they could go through into the yard. From the yard they could if they chose go up into the galleries, paying more money to other gatekeepers at the gallery stairs. In some parts of the galleries there were private rooms, like boxes in a modern theatre. Thus the cheapest part of the house was the open yard where one had to stand, and the customers here were contemptuously called 'Groundlings'. The audience was chiefly of men. Women did sometimes go to the public playhouse, suitably escorted, but generally they were not thought very respectable if they did so. When The Globe was crowded for a popular show it could hold a surprising number of spectators. A full house has been reckoned at about 2,500 people.

An audience at The Globe.

Here then is the time, while the audience are still coming in, to look around us at the setting in which Shakespeare's greatest plays were first put on the stage, under his own direction. Our view is taken from the lower gallery of The Globe, near the main entrance. At each side of the stage are the entrances to the lower gallery, and from there one goes to the stairway entrance beyond, leading to the upper galleries. The gentlemen's boxes are in the lower gallery on each side nearest to the stage. For this performance the gallery over the stage is needed by the actors and by the musicians, who can be seen there, already tuning their instruments, so there are no spectators there, though one or two gentlemen have taken their places on stools at the back of the stage. Let us suppose the play is to be a revival of *The Merchant of Venice,* with Richard Burbage as Shylock. At the back of the stage between the two doors is the curtained enclosure behind which are the caskets for Bassanio's choosing. The musicians above

74

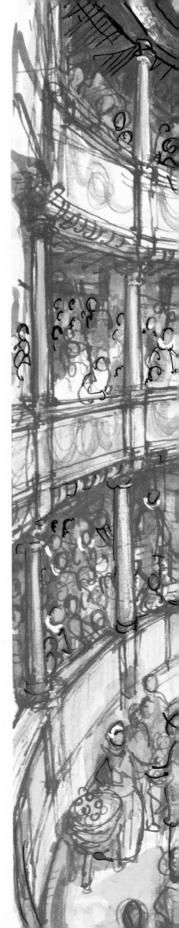

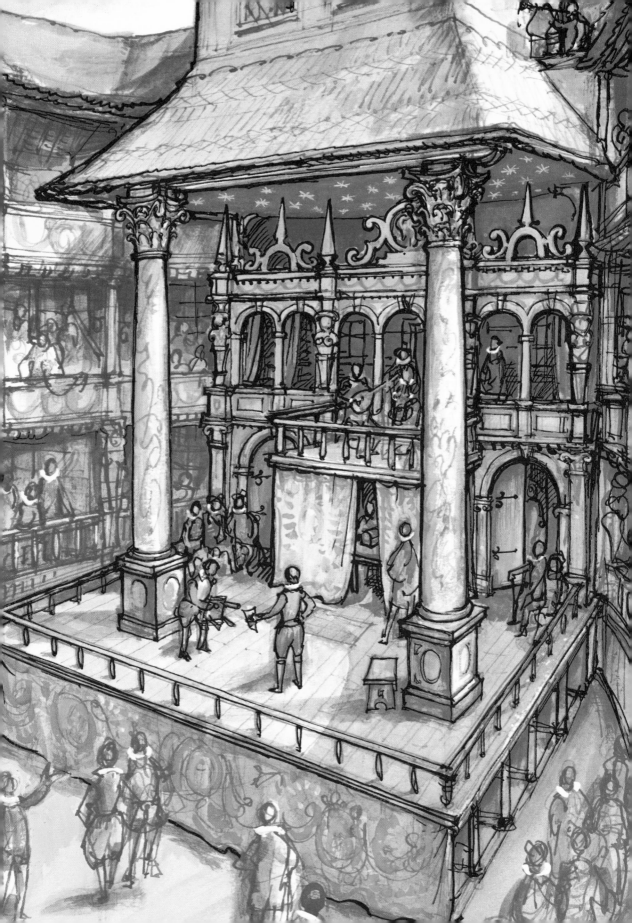

will play for him, while one of them sings 'Tell me, where is fancy bred'. From one of the windows at the side Jessica will throw down the jewels to Lorenzo waiting by the door on the stage below. Some benches, a throne for the Duke of Venice, and a green bank upon which Jessica and Lorenzo will sit to hear the music in the moonlight in Act V, is all the further setting this play requires. But the costumes of the actors, as always, will be grand and colourful. There will be nothing stinted for the Princes of Aragon and Morocco, or Bassanio dressed for his wooing.

In the centre of the stage you may just see the trap door which led down to (or up from) the underneath, the part traditionally known as the 'Hell'. This was often used for the emergence of ghosts or devils, but it had other uses, such as for the grave-diggers in *Hamlet*. Above the stage we see the ceiling of the Heavens, embossed with stars and painted with signs of the Zodiac, and other heavenly devices; and the picture here shows how this was used. A heavenly

A god descends from Heaven.

being, like Jupiter in *Cymbeline,* is descending in a cloud-wrapped throne, to the sound of thunder (a cannon-ball rolled in the loft above) which helps to cover the creaks of the winches which let him down. Above the ceiling and above the whole theatre stands the

A First Sounding.

hut which holds the machinery for all this, and, at the side of the
hut, a man with a trumpet is ready to blow the First Sounding.
This warns us that the players are ready. At the Third Sounding
the play will begin.

78

This was the theatre the professionals had made out of their little travelling stage, with the borrowings of the medieval pageants and many favourite old ideas, such as the old horned Devil and his train. The great days of the amateur were over. In the provincial towns the Mystery Plays one by one were coming to an end, and their amateur performers remained only to be remembered by the professionals in terms of Bottom the weaver, and Snout the tinker, and Flute the bellows-mender, in *A Midsummer Night's Dream*. Far away in the outback the Snake-Man and the Kangaroo-Man continued as always their dedicated play, but in England the play of *Julius Caesar* has now been written. It was in fact performed upon this very stage of The Globe, soon after it was first opened, in September 1599. A German traveller, who was that month in London, saw the play, and wrote a brief account of his visit: ' . . At about 2 o'clock I went over the river with my companions, and in the thatched building saw the Tragedy of the first Emperor Julius Caesar, with at least 15 characters, acted very well.' And he adds later: 'The actors are very expensively and handsomely dressed, for it is an English custom that when distinguished gentlemen or knights die, almost their best clothes are given to their servants; but they, since it is not fitting that they should wear them, sell them cheaply to the actors.' One wonders what clothes he saw the actors wearing in *Julius Caesar,* for, although in those days no attempt was made to give a visual illusion of historical accuracy in dress, as we try to do nowadays on stage and screen, it is likely that the chief characters at least would have been attired in a fashion meant to represent the splendour of an imagined past and the grandeur that was Rome. It will be appropriate here to try to visualize that performance of *Julius Caesar* as our German visitor saw it.

The stage of the Globe before the performance.

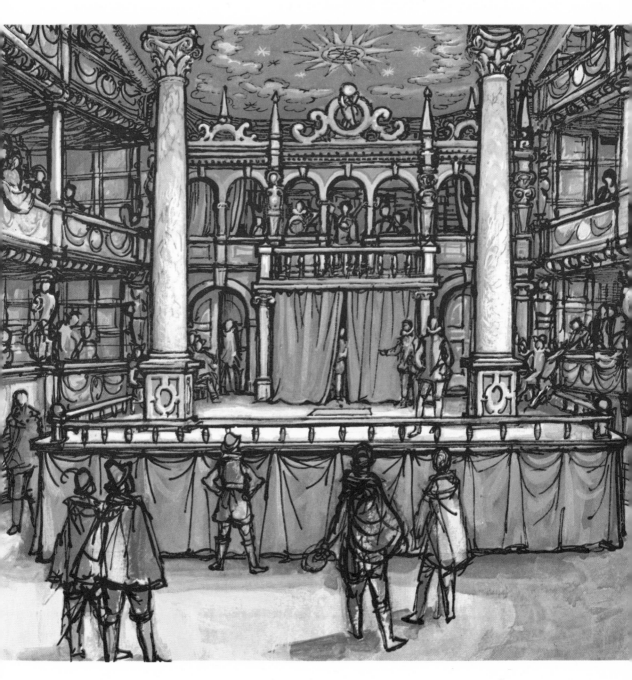

Shakespeare had no taste for special paraphernalia.

The setting of the stage is not very different, except perhaps in a few details of decoration, from that we have just seen prepared for *The Merchant of Venice*. Shakespeare, unlike other authors of his time, had no great need or taste for special paraphernalia. Until the Third Sounding the stage stands empty. Then as the trumpet-note dies away the two doors open on each side of the curtained structure in the centre of the tiring-house wall. From one side the crowd of holidaying citizens come forth, from the other the two tribunes, Flavius and Marullus, who meet the citizens in the centre of the stage, between the posts; and the play begins:

'Hence! Home, you idle creatures, get you home:
Is this a holiday? . . . . . .'

The costumes here are those of Shakespeare's everyday London, but in the next scene there is a change of mood. As the crowd and the tribunes leave the stage, by the door on one side, there is a sound of martial music, and all the principal actors enter in procession

Julius Caesar: the performance in progress.

through the other door, Caesar. Brutus, Cassius and Mark Antony, and the rest, with as many players as can be found to swell the procession, including the musicians. The principals are all dressed in 'Roman' costumes, fanciful and heroic. The scene is short: the soothsayer bids Caesar beware the Ides of March; the procession moves forward again, and having circled the stage goes out by the farther door, leaving Brutus and Cassius alone at the front of the stage to begin the long scene in which Cassius begins to draw Brutus into the conspiracy. Night comes on, as is expressed in the text and in the actions of the players, groping their way through the darkness of the streets, in the afternoon light that comes down from

84

the open ring of sky over the theatre. From within the painted
Heavens overhead a rumbling and rolling sound fills the house—
drums and cannon-balls up there in the loft, but loud thunder down
here in the streets of Rome, where Casca meets Cassius in the storm:

'Who's there?'

'A Roman.'

'Casca, by your voice.'

'Your ear is good. Cassius, what night is this!'

The thunder continues its rumbling over Brutus' orchard, where
the conspirators all meet again 'their hats pluck'd about their ears,
and half their faces buried in their cloaks'. The hats, and the clock
that is heard to strike, are not strictly Roman, but no matter.

The two women's parts of Caesar's wife Calphurnia, and Brutus' wife Portia, are, as is well known, played by boys. One other boy is employed in this play, Brutus' servant Lucius, who in a later act is given a song to sing. The playhouse boy actors must in many cases have been very gifted. It should be remembered that the boys' acting tradition derived from the choir schools of St. Paul's Cathedral and the Chapel Royal, and that boys with well-trained musical voices who had learned to speak Shakespeare's verse just as it was written, if they had any acting talent at all, could hardly fail to be effective. The best of them must have had gifts far beyond this. The parts of Juliet, Rosalind and Cleopatra were not written for actors of little talent. However, the part of Portia in this play needs little more than a well-tuned voice and clear speaking, and is effective as it stands.

The Children of the Chapel Royal performing Lyly's
'Alexander and Campaspe'.

The thunder rolls again as Caesar enters 'in his night gown'. After Calphurnia's warning, which he disregards, he dresses in his state robes on the stage, and goes forth, escorted by his murderers-to-be, to form up within the tiring-house for his last grand procession onto the stage. 'The Ides of March are come,' he says to the soothsayer who meets him midway on the stage. 'Ay, Caesar, but not gone.' The curtained enclosure at the back opens and reveals a throne. Caesar moves towards it and seats himself. The street has transformed itself into the Capitol, and here, shortly, Caesar is stabbed, staggers forward and falls, near the front of the stage, where Antony later comes to lament him: 'O mighty Caesar, dost thou lie so low?'

End of the Tragedy: the funeral march.

There is upon the stage a high place with steps leading up to it, which now will serve as the pulpit in the market place from which Antony will deliver his great oration to the multitude gathered below. This will be spoken not only to the actor citizens of Rome, as many as can be found to fill the stage, but to the crowded groundlings beyond and the audience all around, all equally visible, equally attentive, more than two thousand listening faces in that playhouse afternoon. The pulpit is probably the top of that same curtained space where Caesar's throne had been hidden. This high place, quickly reached from the stage, will be needed again later; and the same curtained enclosure can be used when, in the next Act, after the two opposed armies with their flags and drums have

89

marched out and confronted each other, each from its opposite door upon the stage, Brutus and Cassius retire to their tent for the scene in which they quarrel. Later, in this tent, by candlelight, with Lucius asleep after his song, the ghost of Caesar visits Brutus, and Brutus begins to know his fate.

Swords, shields, drums, flags, marches and countermarches follow. The action sways back and forth, on the stage and off. 'Go, Pindarus, get higher on that hill,' says Cassius, 'and tell me what thou notest about the field.' Pindarus mounts what was once the pulpit in the market place, and is now a hill overlooking the battlefield. He reports ill news. 'Come down, and behold no more,' cries Cassius, 'O coward that I am to live so long!' So the action rolls on to its end. One fancies that it would not be out of keeping with the Elizabethan style of acting, although no stage direction in the text says so, if the ghost of Caesar were to come forth once more, standing perhaps upon the same high place overlooking the battlefield of Philippi, as Brutus, defeated, runs upon his own sword: 'Caesar, now be still; I killed not thee with half so good a will.'

And after the Tragedy, the Jig. 'At the end of the play,' wrote our German visitor, 'two of the actors in men's clothes and two in women's clothes performed a dance, as is their custom, wonderfully well together.' This customary after-piece might also be a rhyming farce on some topical theme, or, as in our picture, a variety of Morris Dance, with a piper and a hobby-horse. And after this the

After the Tragedy, the Jig.

The play is over.

audience would leave. Bankside for a short while would be crowded, as the watermen ferried people back again over the river to the city, as gentlemen called for their horses, and the tiring-house staff began to sort out the properties and costumes for the next day's play.

We should now be able to visualize some scenes in the back-stage area of The Globe. Here is a view in the tiring-house, just behind the stage. The actors are ready. One is making a last minute adjustment to his wig. Backstage is rarely large enough, and this, with all the properties and costumes for such a large repertory of plays to be stored away somewhere, and with so many actors having to find dressing-space wherever they can among the storage, is very crowded indeed. We can see, hanging on a nail on one of the posts, the 'plot' of the play to be performed, a brief synopsis giving the sequence of entrances and the properties required, which serves as a guide to the stage-keeper and his crew, so that every-thing can be got ready in order, a very necessary thing when so many different plays are being done on successive days. A boy is peeping through the curtains to see the state of the house. In

Backstage at The Globe. The tiring-house.

Shakespeare in the tiring-house.

another part of the tiring-house Shakespeare has found himself
space for his writing table, and is making a few revisions necessary
for next week's actors.

Down the tiring-house stairs and under the stage we now find an actor painted ghastly white and dressed in armour, a ghost. This may be the ghost of Hamlet's father, now ready to ascend the steps and rise out of the ground to confront the sentries outside the castle, in the first scene of the play. The two lads are about to open the trap, which will slide back in grooves just above where the

A 'ghost' awaits his cue.

ghost is now standing. Notice the forest of wooden posts that support the stage. In some playhouses the stage was closed in with boards all round, which must have made it very dark, except for whatever daylight could filter through from the doorway by the tiring-house stairs; but where the stage was only hung round with curtains it would still be reasonably light.

Our last backstage scene is in the hut above the stage. The man with the trumpet in the foreground is about to step out onto the little balcony to blow the Third Sounding, but the man at the window beyond, watching for a signal from the auditorium below, is bidding him wait. This hut is divided into two levels. The throne which descends to the stage through the trap-door is at rest on the lower level, and we only see the upper part of it. The trap-door is out of sight beneath. Above, we see the winding gear for this apparatus, and in the background a third man is leaning on one of

The hut above the stage.

the drums of the winch. On the left side two little cannons can be seen. It was customary to shoot off guns as a sign of high spirits in Shakespeare's time, and they were much used in the theatres, not only to simulate battle scenes but also to bump up the background

of festivity. This had an unfortunate result at The Globe, for eventually it burnt the theatre down. It happened during a performance of Shakespeare's *Henry VIII*. There is a scene where the King visits Cardinal Wolsey during a banquet, and at his arrival a salute of cannon is fired. The method used to make the noise was simply to charge the gun with powder, stuff a wadding down the barrel, and light the touch-hole. On this occasion the wadding was shot out blazing, and landed in the thatch of the roof, which, if the cannon were shot from up here, it might easily do. Very soon the whole building was in flames. The fire must have been seen fairly soon, for by good fortune all the audience escaped without injury except for one man who was said to have caught his trousers on fire, but had put out his own flames with a bottle of beer. But The Globe, all thatch and wood, was burnt to the ground. It was rebuilt at once; but the second Globe, though it was reported to have been better built and more magnificent than the first, never achieved the fame of the first one, which was the one for which Shakespeare worked. During the Civil War, with the Puritans in power in London, it was pulled down for good.

It might have been thought that the authorities, who had tried to stop the players coming to London in the first place, had won at last. In a sense they could feel justified. They could point out that public theatres were unsafe. They caught fire during performances; their crowded galleries collapsed and killed the people below; and in days when fear of the plague was never far away, it was known that the spread of infection was particularly dangerous among the close-packed audiences at the playhouse. Moreover, said the Puritans, play-acting, like the May-Pole, was a form of idolatry: and this, if we remember the Snake-Man, and the actors dressed up as saints and angels, and the way in which the very shadows of actors on a screen today can move our own emotions, and especially if we remember the extreme adulation which we give to those of them who are our favourites, was not altogether so silly as it might seem at first. But in spite of all this, and of whatever more might be said against the theatre (as happens whenever a new form of it arises: it has been said against the cinema; it has been said against television) it always turns out somehow that the theatre cannot be suppressed; and this is not simply because people enjoy it, but because they actually *need* it. The theatre is and has always been a necessary part of human life, at all levels, in all parts of the world, and at all times. The Snake- and Kangaroo-men, and the Mummers and Mystery Players, were each performing a human service in play, by making more clear to their watchers the difference between good magic and bad magic, of the nature of sadness and happiness, of right and wrong, and of what we ought to want to be. When the professionals took over from the amateurs, they themselves probably thought very little about such things as this. They probably were chiefly interested in their voices, their styles of acting, and the perfection of their craft. But having perfected it, the next thing that happened was the arrival among them of a man, William Shakespeare, who knew how this craft, now perfected, could best be used to express for larger and larger audiences new and more sensitive ideas about the nature of mankind. The voice of Shakespeare, spoken through the mouths of the actors, remains one of the greatest voices of human experience; and that is why Shakespeare's Theatre, a little thatched building which disappeared long ago, will always be one of the unforgettable places in the history of the human imagination.

INDEX

"A bountifully illustrated, beautiful book, which presents the history of the English theater from its beginnings to the productions of Shakespeare. Starting with the idea that the theater has always been a necessary part of human life, the author describes the survival of ancient pagan rituals in medieval folk dances and festivals; the performances of the 'first professionals'—the traveling jugglers, clowns, and minstrels; then the religious plays of the Church, which became the mystery and miracle cycles performed by amateur actors of the guilds; the influence of the 'professionals' on the secularization of the theater; the traveling players' companies converging upon Elizabethan London; and finally, the building of the permanent playhouses, in particular The Globe. A detailed description of a performance of JULIUS CAESAR gives a vivid picture of the Shakespearean theater—the work of the actors and managers, the settings, costumes, stagecraft, and audiences."   —*Horn Book*